M000296658

Would You Like To 69?

Dearest John,

Thank you for your love, friendship and support throughout the years. You saved my life once upon a time ago, and I'll never forget you.

All my love,

Ida. B. Cumming

This book is a work of fiction. The names, characters and events in this book are the products of the author's imagination or are used fictitiously. Any similarity to real persons living or dead is coincidental and not intended by the author.

The views and opinions expressed in this book are solely those of the author and do not reflect the views or opinions of Gatekeeper Press. Gatekeeper Press is not to be held responsible for and expressly disclaims responsibility of the content herein.

Would You Like To 69?
Published by Gatekeeper Press
2167 Stringtown Rd, Suite 109
Columbus, OH 43123-2989
www.GatekeeperPress.com

Copyright © 2021 by Ida B. Cumming
All rights reserved. Neither this book, nor any parts within it may be sold or reproduced in any form or by any electronic or mechanical means, including information storage and retrieval systems, without permission in writing from the author. The only exception is by a reviewer, who may quote short excerpts in a review.

The cover design and typesetting for this book are entirely the product of the author. Gatekeeper Press did not participate in and is not responsible for any aspect of these elements.

Library of Congress Control Number: 2021936097

ISBN (paperback): 9781662912481

Would You Like To 69?

Ida B. Cumming

gatekeeper press™

Columbus, Ohio

Hello, my name is Candy.
Would you like to 69?

69? 69?

I do not like to 69!

I wonder why you
do not like to 69?

69 is fun, you see.
You should 69 with me!

Would you 69 at the park?
Would you 69 in the dark?

I would not 69 at the park; it doesn't matter if it's dark.
I would not 69 here or there. I would not 69 anywhere.
I do not like to 69!

Could I suck your cock
while on my knees?
We could 69
beneath this tree.

I do not want you on your knees; I will not go beneath that tree.

I would not 69 at the park; it doesn't matter if it's dark.

I would not 69 here or there.

I would not 69 anywhere.

I do not like to 69!

Could you, would you pull my hair?

Give it a yank – I won't care.

I could not, would not pull your hair.

I will not yank it; I do not dare.

I do not want you on your knees.

I will not lie beneath that tree.

I would not 69 at the park;

it doesn't matter if it's dark.

I would not 69 here or there.

I would not 69 anywhere.

I do not like to 69!

Could you, would you lick my box?

I could not, would not lick your box.

I will not pull your hair.

I do not want you on your knees.

I will not lie beneath that tree.

I would not 69 at the park;

it doesn't matter if it's dark.

I would not 69 here or there.

I would not 69 anywhere.

I do not like to 69!

Would you let me tickle your taint,
  causing pleasure so intense you nearly faint?

No, I would not let you tickle my taint! For FUCKS sake,
Candy, have you no restraint?
I would not lick your box.
I will not pull your hair.
I do not want you on your knees.
I will not lie beneath that tree.
I would not 69 at the park;
it doesn't matter if it's dark.
I would not 69 here or there.
I would not 69 anywhere.
I do not like to 69!

I could not 69 in the kitchen. We prepare our food in there, and it isn't sanitary just to mention.
I would not let you tickle my taint.
I would not lick your box.
I will not pull your hair.
I do not want you on your knees.
I will not lie beneath that tree.
I would not 69 at the park;
it doesn't matter if it's dark.
I would not 69 here or there.
I would not 69 anywhere.
I do not like to 69!

I would not 69 in the car, nor in the restaurant
bathroom behind the bar. Jesus Christ, Candy!
You push the boundaries way too far!
I could not 69 in the kitchen.
I would not let you tickle my taint.
I would not lick your box.
I will not pull your hair.
I do not want you on your knees.
I will not lie beneath that tree.
I would not 69 at the park;
it doesn't matter if it's dark.
I would not 69 here or there.
I would not 69 anywhere.
I do not like to 69!

You will like 69. Try it. Try it.
Take my hand, and cum with me.
69 is fun, you'll see.

Candy, if you will let me be,
I will try 69 and you will see
69 is not for me.

a short time later...

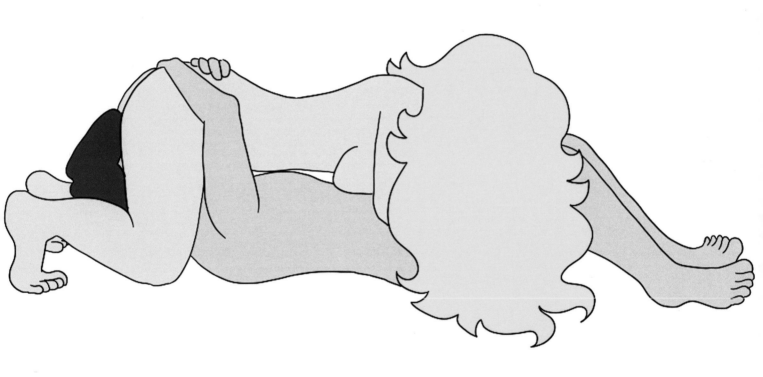

Say, I do like to 69!
You taste fantastic; this is sublime!

I will gladly 69 in the kitchen.

I will happily lick your box

while you fondle and suck my cock.

I would like to grab your hair,

and push your mouth down without a care.

Try not to gag on my dick

while I suckle on your clit.

You can absolutely tickle my taint,

in the dark, at the park, beneath a tree.

69 is so much fun, I see.

So, I will 69 in the car.

I will 69 here or there.

Say, I will 69 anywhere!

But not in the restaurant bathroom behind the bar - too risky.

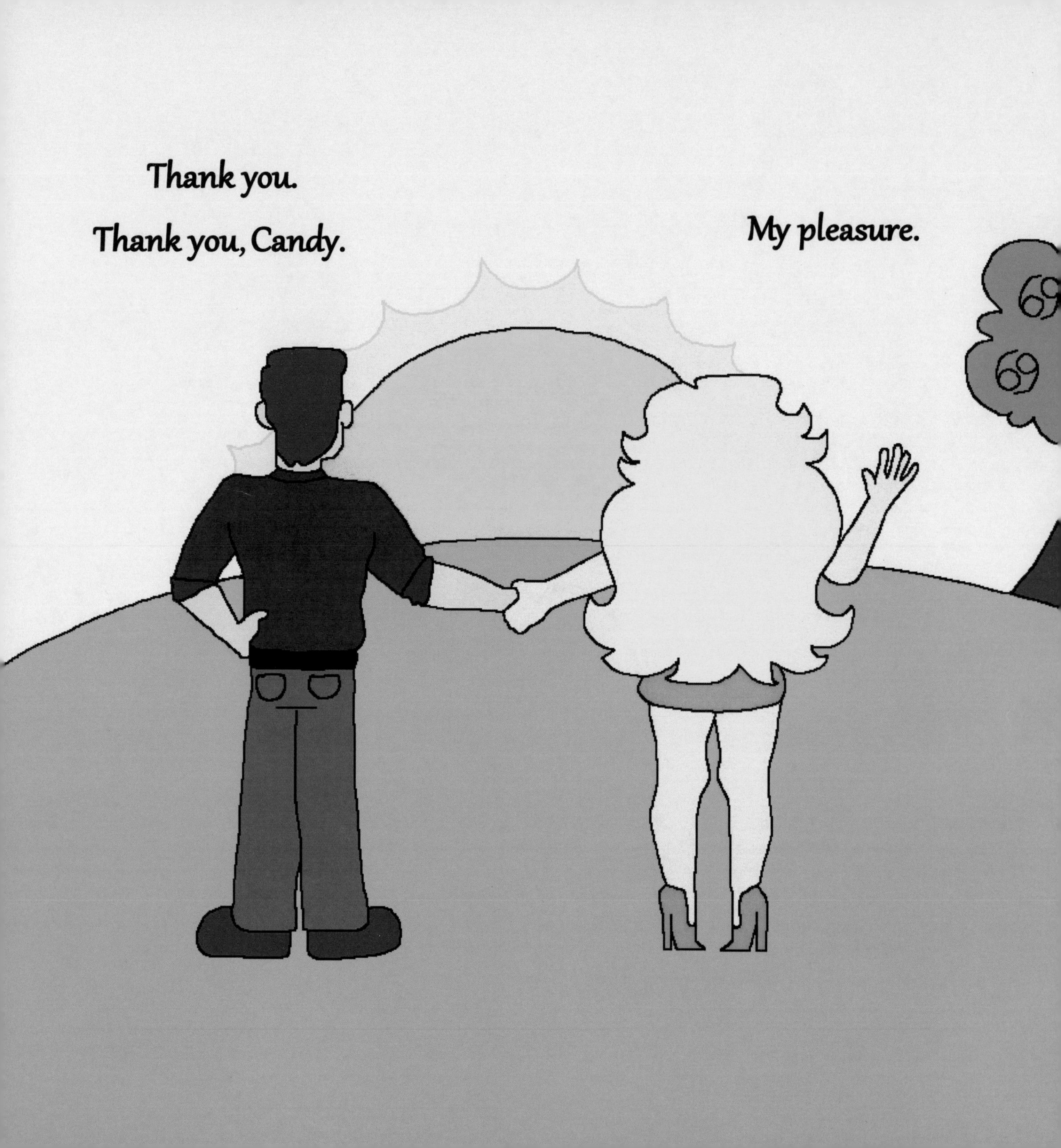
Thank you.
Thank you, Candy.
My pleasure.